FINANCIAL LITERACY
Teens and Young Adults

BEGINNERS
Planning Guide

Money Doesn't Grow on Trees!

by Ashley Gramma

Importance of Finances

It is essential to understand your finances because it helps you not to overspend. Overspending can cause you to get into debt and live paycheck to paycheck. Learning to understand your finances will create awareness and become responsible. You will also learn to make intelligent decisions with

KNOW WHAT YOU ARE SPENDING

Know what you spend each month and plan to make wise choices. Keep a notebook of your monthly spending and decide what your needs and wants are.

Monthly Income:	$
Savings:	$
Rent:	$
Utilities:	$
Groceries:	$
Eating out:	$
Auto Insurance:	$

KNOW YOUR INCOME AND SPENDING

Become aware of your income to be able to make intelligent decisions about your spending. In order to become aware of your income and spending, you will need to make a list of your monthly income, bills, and any other spending. Tracking your income and spending will allow you to see where your money is going.

BUDGETING

BUDGETING AND PLANNING

Budgeting is when you create a plan to help you decide how to spend your monthly income. By budgeting you will learn how to make wise decisions when deciding between needs and wants. In a notebook you should log your spending for a whole month. At the end of the month review the spending log and ask yourself these questions:

What did I spend the most money on?
Are these needs or wants?
What can I cut out of my budget or spend less on?
What can I do make sure I meet my goal and new spending choices?

MONTHLY INCOME & SPENDING TRACKING

You need to know your monthly income, bills, and spending to develop a saving strategy.

Date	What you purchased	Amount spent

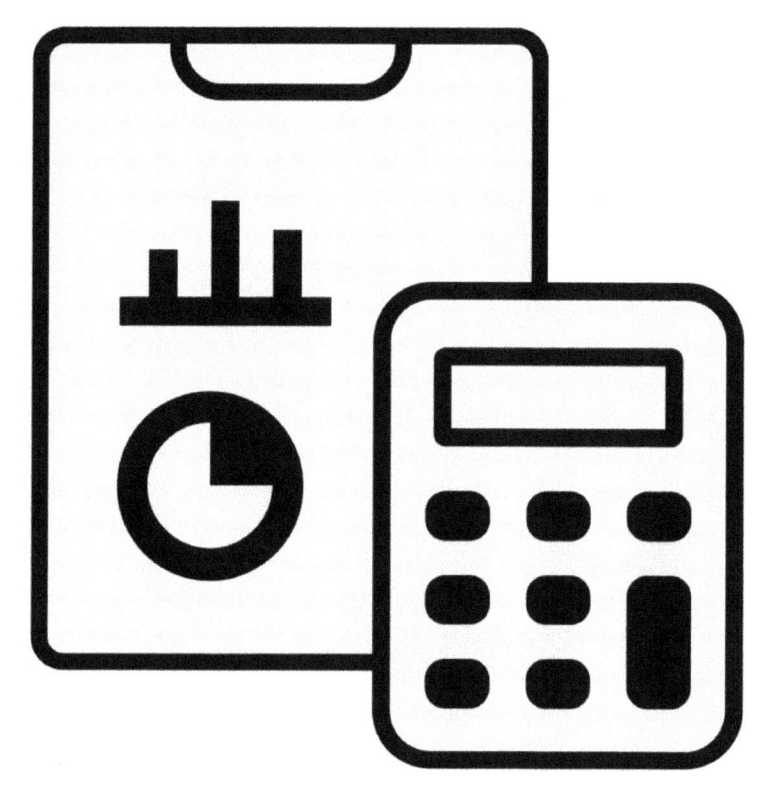

GOAL SETTING

Setting goals are essential when it comes to saving money. You have to keep in mind that you do not have to set significant goals in the beginning. Just know saving is not easy, and you may slip up the first time, but you have to make you keep pushing to do better because it takes lots of practice. Goals can be adjusted if you set them too high. Setting goals and accomplishing them means you are taking charge of your life and learning in the process.

Decision Time

Justify your needs and wants to help you make wise decisions.

Needs	Wants

HOW TO SETUP A BANK ACCOUNT

A bank account is a tool for managing your money. If you are employed, your money can be deposited with ease. Choose a local bank, credit union, or online banking institute. Pick the type of bank account that fits you. Make sure you have two forms of identification and proof of your physical address. You will be required to make a money deposit, and the amount varies depending on the banking institute you choose. You will have to agree to the terms provided in writing, which you should read in detail. If you are under 18 years old, you will need someone over 18 to open the account for you. Having a bank account is a safe place to keep your money, and it is a convenience.

Debit VS Credit

A debit card is a card you receive from your banking institute to spend the money you deposited in that account. You are not able to build credit using a debit card. You are liable for fraudulent purchases and overdraft fees. Debit cards do not charge you interest.

Credit cards allow you to spend limited borrowed money and pay it back later. You use your credit card to make purchases even if you do not have money. The limit is determined based on your credit and income. Credit cards can help build your credit depending on your usage and payment history of the card. Interest will be charged if the bill is not paid in full every month by the due date.

MONEY TIPS:

- Be accountable for your financial actions.
- Organize and track your finances.
- Make saving an automatic habit of yours.
- Pay your bills on time.
- Avoid check-cashing stores and borrowing money from others.
- Save for emergencies.
- Protect yourself and keep your savings amount private. Do not leave your money available to others.
- Use your credit wisely.
- Maintain a job.
- Avoid buying everything new.

Credit Card Issuer	Minimum Authorized User Age
American Express	15
Bank of America	None
Barclays	13
Chase	None
Citibank	None
Discover	15
Synchrony	Varies
US Bank	16
Wells Fargo	None

Parents

Parents can help build their child credit while they are a minor. They have to add them to one other their credit cards as an authorized user, pay the bill on time, and keep the spending on that card under 33 percent. By the time the child is 18 years of age, their credit score can be between 700 to 800 depending on the length of time and spending management of the credit. The parent whose credit is not so good can get a secure credit card by depositing money and crediting against it, and then they can add the child to their credit card as an authorized user.